Going Through the Dry Times

James Ryle

Sovereign World

Sovereign World Ltd
PO Box 777
Tonbridge
Kent TN11 0ZS
England

ISBN 1 85240 305 5

The publishers aim to produce books which will help to extend and build up the Kingdom of God. We do not necessarily agree with every view expressed by the author, or with every interpretation of Scripture expressed. We expect each reader to make his/her judgement in the light of their own understanding of God's Word and in an attitude of Christian love and fellowship.

Cover design by CCD, www.ccdgroup.co.uk
Typeset by CRB Associates, Reepham, Norfolk
Printed in the United States of America

Contents

Foreword

The message in this book is classic. James Ryle writes with such pastoral care and prophetic insight that your soul will drink deeply of the living water being poured out from the heart of God into the hearts of His people. In these inspirational pages you will find answers from heaven for the questions we ask on earth. I love the way James Ryle communicates the truths of God's Word. I am certain you will too.

I must confess that I first read this book in response to a request to write a recommendation for others to read it. In fact, while flying from Pittsburgh to Los Angeles, I thought of at least three or four people who I knew would benefit immediately from the message James was conveying. However, little did I know that the Lord was having me read it for myself! I suspect the same will happen to you in these following pages.

The Bible often illustrates spiritual truth through natural things. For example, the work of the Holy Spirit is sometimes described as being like oil, fire, and water. Jesus on many occasions would use the natural surrounding to make a spiritual point concerning the Kingdom of God. Allegories and parables have always featured significantly in conveying truth to the heart and mind of those seeking after God.

Recently I came across a bit of information showing the human body's need for water. According to the article, more than 70 per cent of the human body consists of water. It takes less than a 1 per cent deficiency in our body's water to make us thirsty. A 5 per cent deficit causes slight fever. An 8 per cent shortage causes the glands to stop producing saliva and the skin to turn blue. A person cannot walk with a 10 per cent deficiency and a 12 per cent deficiency brings death (*Parade Magazine*, August/September, 1998). Now, if this is the case with the natural body's need for water, of how much more importance is it that we have the Water of Life supplying our souls and spirits? As the old hymn says, "I will pour water on him who is thirsty."

In this book, James Ryle shows why the dry times are important and beneficial, but he also opens the floodgates of hope for the Lord's outpouring of grace and mercy into the deep recesses of our very beings! This is not pulp fiction, but the authentic stuff of transparent Christianity. This is a message for all God's servants. It not only provides a sound biblical perspective of the mystery of spiritual dryness, but also charts the path for returning to the Fount of Blessing in the presence of the Lord.

Brace yourself, reader; you are about to have a life-changing encounter with truth that will summon you to a renewed pursuit of Jesus along the River of Life. And so I say to you, in the words of the old spiritual,

"Bones, them bones, them dry bones; now hear the word of the Lord."

Bishop Joseph L. Garlington
Senior Pastor, Covenant Church of Pittsburgh
President of Reconciliation! Ministries International

Author's Preface

We flew into Washington's Dulles International Airport as scheduled. We had about an hour lay over until our flight to Charleston was to depart. A quick cheeseburger and a Coke, a hand or two of Solitaire on the computer, and watching people walk through the airport would help pass the time. Oh yeah, it was raining. Hard.

The agent at the gate made the announcement we were all expecting: "Ladies and gentlemen, we have been advised by flight control there will be a thirty- to forty-minute delay of the flight due to the weather. Please stay in the boarding area in case there is a change."

That sounded promising enough; there was hope we would still make it out of there. However, over the next five hours we continued to be teased with thirty-minute delays until the torture ended at 11.00 p.m. with a blunt and impersonal announcement, "The flight has been cancelled." Did I mention it was raining?

After about an hour of bustling through a crowd of

disturbed travelers, we were able to locate a hotel room for the night and reschedule our flight for the next morning. Everything went according to plan.

On board, as the plane headed for Charleston, I felt a tap on my shoulder by a passenger seated behind me across the aisle. "Aren't you James Ryle?" he asked. "Why, yes," I *humbly* answered (checking out of the corner of my eye to see if he perhaps wanted an autograph).

"I was at Stand in the Gap[1] and heard you preach," he said. "The entire event was an unforgettable experience." I agreed, and then thanked him for his remarks. Our conversation turned to travel. "Where are you headed?" he asked. "Charleston, to do a conference," I replied. I gave him the address of the church where we would be on Sunday, and he said he would try to be there if at all possible. The plane landed and we went our separate ways.

Our visit to Charleston was active, beginning with a Pastors' Luncheon immediately upon our arrival, followed later that night with a Men's Rally Pork-O-Rama BBQ near a river held hostage by mosquitoes. The next morning we played in a golf tournament, and then I preached, and preached, and then preached again. By Sunday morning I was miles away from the plane ride and thoroughly focused on the present task.

Imagine my delight when I saw walking down the aisle in the church the fellow I had met on the plane! He was visibly shaken by the message that morning; there were tears in his eyes, and trembling in his voice. "You will never know what this sermon has done for me today," he said.

As a minister of the gospel I have preached a myriad of sermons over the past several years to a host of people from every walk of life. On occasion there is a sermon of singular importance, noteworthy by its impact upon those who hear it. This book is the fruit of one such sermon. It is the sermon I preached that day in Charleston.

I first preached the message in the late 1980s, and noted then how meaningful it was to so many. My friend John Wimber took a copy of the message and preached it himself on several occasions – always to the deep delight of those who heard him.

To call this sermon timeless would be presumptuous . . . even preposterous. However, the truth it proclaims *is* timeless and worthy of your full consideration. I therefore offer it in writing that you might have it, not only for your edification, but also to share with others who desperately need to hear its hopeful words.

May the Lord bless you through these following pages, and cause your heart to soar with faith in His Word and joy in His presence – though you may sojourn in a dry and weary land where there is no water.

James Ryle

---

[1] On 4 October, 1997 approximately 1.4 million men gathered at the National Mall in Washington D.C. in a solemn assembly. James was asked to preach the gospel at this event.

Chapter 1

Going Through the Dry Times

There is an unmistakable move of the Holy Spirit happening in the world today. A remarkable characteristic of this particular season of blessing is its *diversity*.

Take, for example, the unsettling manifestations and the refreshing joy of the Toronto Blessing, while at the same time we see the deep repentance and dramatic conversions of the Pensacola Revival. Meanwhile, in what seems to be an unrelated thing, men are gathering in stadiums across the nation in unprecedented numbers at Promise Keepers events, and thousands of women are being loosed and set free as Women of Faith in similar settings as well.

The youth are Rocking the Nations for Christ, and world evangelism is experiencing a dramatic upsurge as innumerable converts around the globe turn to Jesus for salvation. In places like Argentina, Brazil and England there are unprecedented stories of remarkable revival and phenomenal healings. At the same time the Alpha Course, an evangelistic tool developed in England, is literally sweeping the world with its user-friendly approach to preaching the gospel.

And the Church, having weathered the scandalous moral failures of prominent ministers and the unrelenting assault of a cynical media, is undergoing profound and positive changes as pastors faithfully provide godly leadership and compelling vision to a people ready to do the work of ministry.

Also, we see an amazing increase of authentic worship as the central part of church life, while at the same time there is an awesome prayer movement sweeping millions of Christians into deeper spirituality and more substantial ministry.

And let's not fail to mention the great strides being made in racial reconciliation, as well as denominational reconciliation. Truly, the walls are coming down! Young and old; men and women; white and black; signs and wonders; repentance and conversion; prayer and worship! Do you see what I mean when I say *diversity*?

Any one of these would be sign enough of the presence and power of the Holy Spirit, but when you consider that they are all occurring *simultaneously* it is a staggering thing. One might easily conclude that the whole Church is caught up in this visitation of God.

But the fact is that many followers of Christ, perhaps the great majority, are experiencing something altogether different. It is yet another example of the diversity of God's work in our midst, and may in fact be the most bewildering sign of them all. I call it "Going through the dry times".

Pass Me Not, O Gentle Savior

Many dear followers of Christ are calling out from the
depths of their hearts the words of the old Gospel
tune:

"Pass me not, O Gentle Savior;
Hear my humble cry.
While on others Thou art calling,
Do not pass me by."

Perhaps you are such a person. Maybe you have
wondered why nothing seems to be happening to
you. Maybe you have traveled from this conference
to that, hoping for one special touch from God that
would let you know you are His special child. And
then, the one conference you decide not to attend is –
of course – the very conference where the mighty
power of God pours out in epic measures and *everybody* is caught up into heaven, healed, delivered,
touched by angels, baptized with fire, and made
wealthy.

Yeah, right.

Perhaps you have prayed earnestly, and dared to
step out in faith for that one touch from God – only to
be left standing when everybody else hits the floor.
You've tried raising your hands, but you feel more silly
than spiritual; you mumbled a few words that you
thought might be tongues, but someone next to you
asked, "Are you clucking like a chicken?" You have
bowed low, jumped high, fasted, cried, hollered and
moaned – and still you are as dry as a bone.

This book is provided in its brevity and simplicity,

in the hope of giving assurance and peace to those who seem to be left out while God is zapping everybody else. In other words, this book is for *you*.

A Note of Clarification

A note of clarification is in order before we proceed. It will be helpful to state what we do *not* mean when we speak about *"going through the dry times"*.

We are not talking about that inevitable darkness of thought and dullness of heart that comes as the result of our deliberate disobedience to the Lord. If you are presently in a spiritual mess because you have resisted the leading of the Holy Spirit, or have done something you know was contrary to the will of God – this is not going through the dry times. You are being disciplined by the Lord, who loves you too much to leave you the way you are.

When David tried to hide his sin he became tormented and cried out to God:

> *"Have mercy upon me, O LORD, for I am in trouble: mine eye is consumed with grief, yea, my soul and my belly. For my life is spent with grief, and my years with sighing: my strength faileth because of mine iniquity, and my bones are consumed."* (Psalm 31:9–10 KJV)

On another occasion he says:

> *"When I kept silence, my bones waxed old through my roaring all the day long. For day and night thy hand*

*was heavy upon me: my moisture is turned into the
drought of summer."*   (Psalm 32:3–4 KJV)

The deliberate pressure brought by God's love for
David led him to repentance and confession of his
sin. This proved to be the turning point in his spiritual
drought. Listen to his own testimony as he speaks to
us down the corridor of time:

*"All day and all night your hand was heavy on me. My
strength evaporated like water on a sunny day until I
finally admitted all my sins to you and stopped trying
to hide them. I said to myself, 'I will confess them to
the Lord.' And you forgave me! All my guilt is gone.
Now I saw that each believer should confess his sins
to God when he is aware of them, while there is time to
be forgiven. Judgment will not touch him if he does."*
        (Psalm 32:4–6 TLB)

Friend, I appeal to you to follow David's example.
Turn to the Lord and be honest about what you have
done. He will forgive and restore you, and show the
way through your dark valley to Zion's glorious
mountains. Do this even now, before going any
further. Your Father awaits your return!

Also, there may be someone whose "loss of joy"
stems not from a dry time orchestrated by grace, but
rather from *burn out.* You have tried too hard to do too
much for too long and have simply worn yourself to a
frazzle. You may find chapter 5 to be the best news
you've read in a long time.

And then there may be those who through ignor-
ance, neglect or sloth have let slip through their hands

the sweet fruit of fellowship with the Lord – which was given in its season to be your supply for the moment, and to sustain you for the journey. Now, though empty handed, don't act as if you are empty headed!

The Lord is slow to anger and great in mercy and forgiveness. He also has an abundance of fruit and a very generous disposition to His repentant children. Turn to Him now and ask in faith for renewal of your affections, and restoring of your possessions.

He will hear you and answer from heaven!

Now then, onward through this desert to the hope of better things!

Chapter 2

The Desert of Judah

David, a man after God's own heart, prayed:

> *"O God, you are my God,*
> *earnestly I seek you;*
> *my soul thirsts for you,*
> *my body longs for you,*
> *in a dry and weary land*
> *where there is no water.*
> *I have seen you in the sanctuary*
> *and beheld your power and your glory.*
> *Because your love is better than life,*
> *my lips will glorify you.*
> *I will praise you as long as I live,*
> *and in your name I will lift up my hands."*
> (Psalm 63:1–4 NIV)

Commenting on this psalm, Spurgeon wrote:

> "David did not leave off singing because he was
> in the wilderness, neither did he in slovenly idle-
> ness go on repeating Psalms intended for other

occasions. Rather, he carefully made his worship suitable to his circumstances, and presented to his God a wilderness hymn when he was in the wilderness."

This song is interesting for many reasons. First, it encompasses present, past and future. David says:

"... God, you are my God,
  earnestly I seek you;
my soul thirsts for you,
  my body longs for you,
in a dry and weary land
  where there is no water."

That was his *present* condition when he wrote the song. He was faced with the difficulty of dryness, yet he did not lose sight of the fact that God was *his* God. This is a present-tense relationship. Perhaps your own season of dryness should be characterized with a similar confession of faith: "God, You are my God." It is, after all, the truth.

Then David says,

"I have seen you in the sanctuary
  and beheld your power and your glory."

This is *past* tense. There was a time, glorious and unforgettable, when David beheld the beauty of the Lord and inquired in His holy Temple; a time when he danced with all his might and worshipped in the beauty of holiness. It is good to remind ourselves during the dry times of just what we have seen and known of the Lord in times past.

Can you recall a time when the Lord's presence was real and near, a time when you were enthusiastic in worship and service? That time was valid, and your present dryness does not negate the gains that were made for Christ when the river flowed freely. Just because you are dry does not mean you are dead. Pause for a moment and reflect upon those life-impacting encounters you have had with the Lord in the past. Let their memory be the momentum that carries you forward through this valley.

And then David looks in faith to the *future* when he writes:

> *"Because your love is better than life,*
>   *my lips will glorify you.*
> *I will praise you as long as I live,*
>   *and in your name I will lift up my hands."*

This future hope shows us that we go *through* the dry times; we are not left *in* them. A better day is coming; the Lord will not leave me in this dry and weary land where there is no water.

You can be like the old lady who told the preacher her favorite promise in the Bible was, *"It came to pass."* When the preacher asked, "What do you mean?" she replied, "When troubles or dark moments of sorrow and difficulty come my way, I just remember the word *'It came to pass,'* and I know it won't be long before it's over!"

Know this about the dry time you are in – it came to

pass! (By the way, this is equally true of those seasons when everything is bubbly and wonderful!)

The second fascinating fact of this song is that David wrote it in the Desert of Judah. We most often associate the desert with the wilderness between Egypt and the Promised Land. Egypt was a place of dreaded bondage, and the desert was a place where the people wandered for forty years in sin and unbelief. But the Promised Land flowed with milk and honey, abundant in fertile soil and rich crops, copious in fruit and wine, and teeming with unending prosperity.

So, what is this *Desert* of Judah? Isn't Judah a part of the Promised Land? How can there be a desert in a land that flows with milk and honey? More to the point is this fact: if you're going through a dry time, it doesn't mean you are not in God's will. You see, there is a wilderness in the Promised Land: a desert in Judah!

A Lesson for Us Today

The Bible teaches us as Christians that the things that happened to the Israelites in their journey of faith hold much instruction for us in ours. Paul says,

> *"Now these things happened to them as an example, and they were written for our instruction, upon whom the ends of the ages have come."*
> (1 Corinthians 10:11 NASB)

Could it be that just as there was a desert in the Promised Land for them, so there is one for us as well? Could it be that going through the dry times is every bit as much God's will for us as our being swept up in the mighty outpouring of the River of Life? Is it possible that those who are dry and seasoned with sand are as much in the center of God's will as those who are being slain in the Spirit, laughing with joy unspeakable, and doing mighty things for God?

I think so.

Common to Us All

The simple truth is this: the desert experience is *common* among believers. We all find our paths winding through its dry and demanding terrain. Spurgeon said,

> "A weary place and a weary heart make the presence of God the more desirable. How frequently have believers traversed in their experience this dry and thirsty land."

Moses saw God in the wilderness, as did Elijah, David and Paul. And don't lose sight of the fact that Jesus Himself *"was led by the Spirit into the desert to be tempted by the devil"* (Matthew 4:1 NIV).

> "Every devout soul, which has loved to see God in His house, will be refreshed by visions of God in the wildernesses of solitude and sorrow."
> (Christopher Wordsworth)

Take heart, O dry bones; the desert experience is indeed common to all believers.

Common also is how easily we misunderstand the purposes of God during those dry times when the lights go out. Because we misunderstand His purposes, we often miss the blessings He is bestowing into our lives during these profound and priceless moments.

Isaiah the prophet asked an interesting set of questions to a bewildered people.

> *"Who among you fears the LORD?*
> *Who obeys the voice of His Servant?*
> *Who walks in darkness*
> *And has no light?"*   (Isaiah 50:10a NKJV)

This doesn't seem right. Is it possible to fear the Lord, obey His word, and yet walk in darkness and have no light? It must be, seeing how so many of us experience this. But we can take heart, for Isaiah offers this counsel,

> *"Let him trust in the name of the LORD*
> *And rely upon his God."*   (Isaiah 50:10b NKJV)

Don't get nervous and fretful when the Lord doesn't seem to be as near and dear as in times past. Be patient and continue trusting in the Lord, even when you don't *feel* as if it is making any difference.

Isaiah also gives a sober warning to those who try to light their own fire when God turns the lights out.

> *"Look, all you who kindle a fire,*
> *Who encircle yourselves with sparks:*
> *Walk in the light of your fire,*
> *   and in the sparks you have kindled –*

This you shall have from My hand:
You shall lie down in torment."

(Isaiah 50:11 NKJV)

Sometimes the Lord turns the lights out and causes us to pass through dry times to give us the opportunity of trusting in Him apart from feeling or fancy. It would be a mistake to generate a fake experience of spirituality during such times.

You Shall Know the Truth

The simple truth is that the desert is not a place of punishment or abandonment by God; rather, it is a place of great promise and amazing potential – as I will show in the following pages. Failure to understand this sets us up for an assault from Satan, the enemy of our souls. He assails us during the dry times more than any other, because he knows it is when we are the most vulnerable.

The devil thrives on taking advantage of us during times when the Lord is silent and our way is hard. He wants us to doubt God's love and faithfulness, and to second-guess our security in Christ. He wants us to whisper and murmur, soliciting from others – who themselves are low – unholy counsel and dishonest support. Misery loves company. The devil wants us to become anxious, fretful and self-motivated in our desperation to do something to change our circumstances. He wants us to fall into sin, and to bring dishonor to the Lord.

Certainly these are the kinds of things the devil is up

to all the time, but he definitely intensifies the attacks along these lines when we are going through dry times. However, he can only succeed if we remain ignorant.

The prophet Hosea wrote,

> *"My people are destroyed for lack of knowledge."*
> (Hosea 4:6 NASB)

Jesus said,

> *"Then you will know the truth, and the truth will set you free."* (John 8: 32 NIV)

Notice here that it is not the truth that sets us free: rather, it is the truth we *know*. If you don't know it, then the truth will not make any difference in your life or circumstances. The devil knows this, and is set on keeping you from knowing the truth and experiencing the freedom that only Christ can give.

Let me help you in the following chapters to discover five uplifting truths about going through the dry times. Knowing them will help you navigate your way safely through the wilderness as you press on upwards, seeking that city whose builder and maker is God.

Chapter 3

Fact No. 1 –

The Desert
is a Place of *Testing*

"Remember how the LORD your God led you all the way in the desert these forty years, to humble you and to test you in order to know what was in your heart, whether or not you would keep his commands."

(Deuteronomy 8:2 NIV)

From one perspective it can be safely argued that the Jews *wandered* in the wilderness for forty years. That is a matter of historical and chronological fact.

But Moses gives us an entirely different perspective to consider when he says, *"Your God led you all the way in the desert these forty years."* Here we discover they weren't *wandering* at all; they were being *led*. This implies purpose and direction. Where was God leading them, and *why*? Moses tells us: *"to humble you and to test you in order to know what was in your heart, whether or not you would keep his commands."*

Why, God?

Have you ever wondered why God does some of the things He does? Here is one such case. God led them in the wilderness to humble and to test them, in order to know what was in their hearts. Did God *not* know? Did He need the heat of the desert to reveal something in their hearts that they had successfully hidden from Him? Of course not! Certainly God knew what was in their hearts; He knew whether or not they would obey Him. So what does this mean?

I once heard a preacher say, "When God asks a question, it is not because He needs to know the answer. Rather, He wants you to hear the answer that you give, and to consider it from God's point of view." For example, "Adam, where are you?" (see Genesis 3:8ff.). Obviously God knew, but He wanted Adam to know. He wanted Adam to consider why he was hiding from God, and to answer in humility and honesty. Another example is, "Cain, where is your brother, Abel?" (see Genesis 4). God knew. He wanted Cain to see what he had done from God's point of view.

So it is here in this case. God led them in the wilderness those forty years for *their* sake, not His. He wanted them to see things from His point of view. God often puts us in situations that are too much for us, so that we will learn there is no situation that is too much for Him.

Furthermore, they needed to know what was in their hearts, whether or not they would obey the Lord. Thomas à Kempis wrote,

"Adversities do not make a man frail; they show what sort of man he is."

In other words, adversity introduces a man to himself. In another place à Kempis wrote,

"It is very expedient for thy welfare that thou be left sometimes without taste of spiritual sweetness, and in a dry condition; lest perhaps thou should be vain about thy prosperous estate, and should be willing to please thyself in that which thou art not."

The scripture says that God leads you through the wilderness *"to humble you and to test you in order to know what was in your heart, whether or not you would keep his commands."* God humbles us so that our confidence will be in Him alone. God tests us, not so that we will fail, but so that we will succeed. He is inspecting us during these dry times with a view to giving us His *approval* – not rejecting us. He wants to reveal our strengths, not our weakness.

Finally, God led them through the wilderness not so much to put them in the Promised Land, but to put the Promised Land in them. In other words, it is not enough to want simply to get out of Egypt: we must also want to enter our Promised Land.

I heard A.R. Bernard say,

"A man without a vision is a man without a future. And a man without a future will always revert to his past."

God led the children of Israel into the desert to give them a vision for the Promised Land. He took them out of Egypt so that He could take Egypt out of them – and put a longing in their hearts for the Promised Land. They had to *want* it before they could *have* it. The Apostle James summed this up when he wrote, *"you do not have because you do not ask"* (James 4:2 NKJV).

It is the same with us today. We must ask in order to receive. So what does God do to ensure our asking? He takes us into the desert! It is not only the quickest way to the Promised Land, it is also the *only* way out of Egypt.

J.B. Phillips wrote:

> "Christ made no promise that those who followed him in his plan of re-establishing life on its proper basic principles would enjoy a special immunity from pain and sorrow – nor did he himself experience such immunity. He did, however, promise enough joy and courage, enough love and confidence in God to enable those who went his way to do far more than survive."

Indeed, to prevail.

'Twas the Week Before Christmas

An unusual trial befell me several years ago. It started on the Tuesday before Christmas, which was on Sunday that year. I woke up into what I can only call the *absence* of the Lord. Now I know He said, *"I will*

never leave you, or forsake you" (Hebrews 15:5 NRSV),
but at that moment I could not find Him anywhere;
not in the Scripture, nor in prayer; not in song, nor in
confession of faith. He was *gone.*

I made it through the day thinking that this was a
test of some kind, and that it would pass rather
quickly. But the next morning when I awoke, the
feeling of emptiness had intensified, and I was deeply
troubled at the thought that this may be for real ...
and *for ever.*

By the following morning my fears were strengthened, as the problem grew even worse. Each day
seemed to multiply my sense of being totally lost. By
Saturday morning I groped about like a man who had
never known the Lord at all. There was no discernible
trace of His Spirit, His grace, or the power of His Word
in my life. I was alarmed, to say the least.

To make matters worse, Sunday was coming. I was
frantic in my search for some meaningful sermon to
preach on Christmas Day, but could find nothing – a
preacher's worst nightmare. I covered my tracks by
having the children take the morning service and sing
to the congregation a variety of carols and hymns. As
for myself, I left the church before the service ended
and raced home to hide in my bedroom!

Monday morning dawned and my greatest fears
were realized. The ordeal was relentless, and my sense
of emptiness was more intense than ever. I dreaded
the thought of what my future held, for I clearly
would not be able to continue as a pastor in this
condition.

However, the next morning when I woke, the Lord
was present in a manifest way there in my room. I

literally gasped like a man coming up out of water after almost drowning. With the exhale of that breath of life, I blurted out a tangled prayer that sounded something like, "Lord, where have You ... what was this ... and, please, don't ever do that again!"

The Lord opened my heart to understand what He had been doing. Into my mind came the phrase, "The Lord is taking me from the minor leagues to the major leagues." In other words, He showed me that He was about to increase His anointing in my life, and with that would come greater influence and responsibility in ministry. The dark ordeal was a portal of testing that led from one level to the next.

I wrote a little poem to commemorate that moment.

'Twas the Week Before Christmas

" 'Twas the week before Christmas
  and all through my house
The Lord was not moving
  I felt like a louse!
My prayers were like cement,
  my faith was like mud;
My spirit was sinking;
  my life was a dud!
So with desperate endeavor
  I hastened to see
Just what in the world
  was happening to me!
I called on the Name
  of the Lord God Most High!
And with speed like molasses
  He finally replied...

'This week is a test
  I'm passing you through;
I'm weighing your heart
  to see what you'll do.
For I've purposed to use you
  in ways I think best,
But I only can do so
  if you pass this test!' ''

Did I pass the test? I don't know. Personally I don't think I handled it so well, but I can only say this in retrospect. Shortly after that incident I became the chaplain for the University of Colorado football team, and a close friend to Bill McCartney. In a few short months from those first days of my new adventure, the Lord unleashed His Spirit and brought the Promise Keepers Movement into being; and He was pleased to have me take part in the work.

Now, at the time of writing, I have been privileged to preach the gospel to over two million men in the past few years, and untold thousands have come to Christ as Savior and Lord! To God be the glory, great things He has done!

Paul writes,

"but just as we have been approved by God to be entrusted with the gospel, so we speak, not as pleasing men but God, who examines our hearts."
(1 Thessalonians 2:4 NASB)

I see a defined pattern here revealing a divine process: first God examines our hearts, then He approves us to be entrusted with the gospel. Finally, we speak in a

manner that pleases God, and God backs us up.
Simply stated – God *tests* us; then He *trusts* us; and
then He *entrusts* us with the gospel and His power in
preaching it.

Maybe the dry time you are going through is the
Lord's way of preparing you for a season of extraordinary blessing and usefulness. Maybe you are being
tested, so that you can be trusted – and then entrusted
with the awesome privilege of co-laboring with Christ
in these days of unprecedented opportunity!

Maybe so.

Chapter 4

Fact No. 2 –
The Desert
is a Place of *Growth*

"And the child grew and became strong in spirit; and he lived in the desert until he appeared publicly to Israel." (Luke 1:80 NIV)

When God wants to make a cucumber, He takes about six weeks. When He wants to make an oak, He takes about twenty years. What do you think He is making of *you?*

It seems He is in no hurry when it comes to the growth of His children. His principal work is that we mature into men and women of Christlike character and conduct in this world. Such maturity demands that we be weaned from a dependence upon spiritual euphoria.

Consequently, there come into our lives – by the will of God – seasons of spiritual inactivity, boredom, setbacks, frustration and confusion. At issue here is this: are we loving and serving God simply because of how wonderful it makes us feel to do so? Or do our motives have a nobler end? Indeed, shouldn't they?

As, Gary L. Thomas, founder of the Center for Evangelical Spirituality, wrote,

> "Without the desert experience we could very easily settle in a place where we enjoy the fruits of worshipping God (i.e., our *feelings*) more than we enjoy the God we worship."

Also, without significant dry times humbling and testing us, it is likely that we could become puffed up with a false sense of our own legendary spirituality. Can't you recall those first days of faith when you were born again? All things seemed possible; you were ready to save the world! Then, after the initial season of discovery and delight, didn't it happen to you as it does to many others? First, there is a subtle sense of slight spiritual superiority and smugness, followed by the need to make others aware of just how much you know. This in turn leads to an attitude of judgement and fault-finding with others who, in your opinion, aren't as devoted as you.

Ah, the desert can put the squeeze on such thinking quicker than anything! And thus, the Lord ordains for us those necessary droughts to bring us down a peg or two. The Psalmist wrote:

> *"Lord, I am not proud and haughty. I don't think myself better than others. I don't pretend to 'know it all.' I am quiet now before the Lord, just as a child who is weaned from the breast. Yes, my begging has been stilled."*   (Psalm 131:1–2 TLB)

God must wean us from a childish preoccupation with our need for nurture, in order to mature us with a compelling sense of destiny and significance.

Nurture and *destiny*. These two requirements must be balanced in our lives or else everything ends up out of sorts. When all we seek is nurture, we remain childish and co-dependent. If all we ever think about is destiny, we become short-tempered and obsessive with achievement.

God wants to balance our lives with nurture and destiny. He must first wean us from the breast and then lean us on His chest. Dry times serve His purpose best in this intrepid transition. Then, like the prodigal who went through his own dry time, we no longer demand, "Father, *give* me my portion of the inheritance!" Rather, we humbly say, "Father, *make* me whatever pleases You." "*Give* me" is nurture; "*make* me" is destiny.

The psalmist made it clear that humility is the fruit of being weaned. *"Lord, I am not proud and haughty,"* he wrote, adding, *"my begging has been stilled."* From begging to giving; from pride to humility – that's what God does by taking us through dry times.

Humility is the God-given self-assurance that eliminates the need to prove to others the worth of who you are and the rightness of what you do. God leads us through the desert to put this kind of humility in our hearts.

Becoming Strong in Spirit

It was said of John the Baptist that *"the child grew and*

became strong in spirit; and he lived in the desert" (Luke 1:80 NIV). Notice that his growth was primarily *spiritual*.

No growth is complete that leaves out spiritual development. I often heard Bill McCartney tell his football team, "The spiritual is to the physical as four is to one." By this he meant that a man with his spirit set right by God had far more going for him than a man with nothing but muscles. Take a guy who is physically fit and infuse him with the Holy Spirit – you have a formidable package! That's what John the Baptist was like.

Notice the scripture goes on to say of John, *"he lived in the desert until he appeared publicly to Israel."* Hmmm. I wonder if the Lord sometimes puts us in the desert in order to have us grow and become strong in spirit. It certainly would seem so, looking at John as an example.

A gem is not polished without rubbing, nor are godly men and women made without trials. Think about it. Haven't the greatest strides in your spiritual journey always come during times of significant difficulty and hardship?

> "Many men and women owe the grandeur of their lives to their tremendous difficulties."
>
> (C.H. Spurgeon)

John was in the desert until it was the right time for him to appear to Israel. Might not the same be true of you? This pattern certainly holds true for many of God's champions.

Paul was himself in the desert for three years, and

then sidelined in Antioch for fourteen years before the Lord brought him into his apostolic ministry. Joseph endured the hostilities of false accusation and unjust imprisonment long before God exalted him throughout Egypt. Moses tended sheep for forty years before leading the children of Israel out of Egyptian bondage and into history. David was faithful in the unseen and uncelebrated duties of ordinary labor, and there secretly slew a lion and a bear, long before God brought him out publicly to slay Goliath and lead a nation. It seems clear enough that God uses the dry and desperate times in the desert to effect a spiritual maturity in our lives.

Francis de Sales, when he was nineteen, experienced a dreadful fear of eternal damnation. He thought certainly that God had indeed destined him for hell. He lived with this torment for several weeks until he finally cried out to God, "If I may not love Thee in the other world – for in hell none shall praise Thee – let me at least spend every moment of my brief life here in loving Thee as much as I can." As he finished praying the torment left him and he was fully recovered to a vibrant faith and love of God. Forever thereafter he was renowned for his deep understanding and enduring patience with suffering souls. He had grown through the awful ordeal, and became the man he could not have been before.

Jesus is our best example of patient growth during unnoticed years of quietness and apparent inactivity. Luke writes of Jesus that He *"grew in wisdom and stature, and in favor with God and men"* (Luke 2:52 NIV). Mentally, physically, spiritually and socially – these are four areas of life in which God wants us to experience healthy, balanced growth. Are you growing in these areas? In which one would you say you are the most undeveloped? Might this season of dryness be a gift to you from the Lord to develop that one area?

A lesson from nature will suffice here to make a simple point. Healthy growth requires shade as much as sunshine. A plant needs the dry season, as well as the rain. If this is true of plants, might it also be true of you and me? Could it be that God is effecting a significant transformation of your life during this season of disconsolate dryness and seeming barrenness? I think so.

Healthy Things Grow

Here is a formula I developed some time ago, which many have found to be very helpful in assessing just where they are in this thing called spiritual growth. Perhaps you will find it useful in your life as well. It consists of seven simple facts, each one leading to the next in a natural and inevitable sequence.

► **Fact one:** *healthy things grow*

If you want to be healthy, you need to grow. This is a fact of life, whether it be people, plants, businesses, marriages, churches, investments or whatever: if it is healthy, it will grow.

► **Fact two:** *growing things change*

This is how we know they are growing. They are different from when we last saw them.

▶ Fact three: *changing things challenge us*

Mark Twain said, "The only person that likes change is a wet baby." Basically, we want things to stay the way we like them. We are creatures of habit and comfort, and so prefer things to be left alone when we have them just the way we think they ought to be. When change happens, it presents us with challenge. The greater the change, the greater the challenge.

▶ Fact four: *challenging things force us to trust God*

I mean, what else are you going to do – *quit?* Challenge requires that we trust God, especially when we are faced with something that seems to be more than we can handle.

Here is a thought: "A test is not a test until it's a test!" In other words, God knows your limits. He knows exactly where to apply the pressure to cause you to turn to Him in faith. What might be a test for someone else may be a walk in the park for you – and vice versa. It is not a *test* until it forces you to turn to God in simple trust.

▶ Fact five: *trust leads to obedience*

The old Gospel songwriter said it best, "Trust and obey, for there's no other way to be happy in Jesus but to trust and obey." If we truly trust the Lord, He will reveal His will to us; He will show us what to do. Thus, trust leads to obedience. The only question now is, will we obey?

▶ **Fact six:** *obedience makes us healthy*

Jesus said,

> *"Take my yoke upon you, and learn from me, for I am gentle and humble in heart, and you will find rest for your souls. For my yoke is easy and my burden is light."*   (Matthew 11:29–30 NIV)

When we obey the Lord, His joy floods our souls and His peace fills our lives. There is no rest for the wicked, but those who do God's will find their lives filled with blessing.

▶ **Fact seven:** *healthy things grow*

Now we are back to where we started. That's how it works; it is the cycle of spiritual growth every child of God experiences. Even now you are somewhere in this cycle – that is, if you want to be *healthy*. Review these seven phases and consider where you are in the process. You'll end up in a good place, praising God for bringing you through it all.

Gary L. Thomas writes:

> "Having passed through the desert we are not so easily shaken. Strong feelings no longer move us. We may still enjoy them, but they do not over-whelm us; they do not direct us. We have learned to submit our will to God, to be moved by truth and His Spirit. Spiritual feelings are no longer our Seeing Eye dogs, but rather little Chihuahuas dancing at our feet."
>
> (*Seeking the Face of God*, Harvest, p. 197)

Perhaps this short poem says it best for all of us:

"Light after darkness, gain after loss;
   Strength after weakness, crown after cross;
Sweet after bitter, hope after fears;
   Home after wandering, praise after tears;
Sheaves after sowing, sun after rain;
   Sight after mystery, peace after pain;
Joy after sorrow, calm after blast;
   Rest after weariness, sweet rest at last;
Near after distance, gleam after gloom;
   Love after loneliness, life after tomb;
After long agony, rapture of bliss;
   Right was the pathway, leading to this."

(Anon)

Chapter 5

Fact No. 3 –
The Desert
is a Place of *Rest*

*"Then, because so many people were coming and going
that they did not even have a chance to eat, he said to
them, 'Come with me by yourselves to a quiet place
and get some rest.'"* (Mark 6:31 NIV)

As one preacher said, *"Come apart before you come
apart!"* There are times in every life when the greatest
of all needs is quiet withdrawal. Harvest, to be most
plentiful, requires shadow as much as sunshine.

The disciples were in the midst of a busy ministry
experience; non-stop service in the cause of Christ.
And yet it was Jesus who said, *"Come with me by
yourselves to a quiet place and get some rest."*

The Lord Knows Our Limits

He knows what extended stretches in ministry without rest and relaxation will do to us. Therefore, He has

ordained these seasons of repose to provide us with the opportunity of reflecting upon all that has been accomplished by the grace of God, and to be replenished for upcoming seasons of even more victories and advances of faith.

You may be going through the dry time for no other reason than this – the Lord wants you to take a break and enjoy life at an easier pace! Play golf, go fishing, read books, bowl – *whatever.* Just don't minister!

Yes, the Lord said, *"Go into all the world and preach the good news"* (Mark 16:15 NIV) – but your dry time is saying, "Not right now!" We can't preach the good news and *be* the bad news! Furthermore, one cannot give away what one does not have. If your soul is not at rest, how can you expect to call others to enter into the rest of the Lord?

Could it be your compulsive need to minister is rooted in something less than noble? Might all your puff and stuff be nothing more than an attempt to make yourself look more spiritual than you really are, or to meet an unfulfilled internal need for approval or acceptance?

Not only does the Lord know our limits, He also knows the vanity of our selfish thoughts. He knows how prone we are to serve so as to make a good showing of our spirituality, to impress others with our devotion and faithfulness – as well as to show them up for their lack of the same.

"Busyness" is our way of appearing important and significant. Maybe the dry spell is God's way of toning us down, of bringing us back into focus, by showing us that we are not as indispensable as we may suppose.

John Maxwell, a friend of mine, often shares this quaint poem about the "Indispensable Man":

"Sometime when you're feeling
    important.
Sometime when your ego's in bloom.
Sometime when you take it for granted
    you're the best qualified in the room.
Sometime when you feel your departure
    would leave an unfillable hole.
Just follow these simple instructions
    and see how it humbles your soul.
Take a bucket and fill it with water.
    Put your hand in it up to the wrist.
Pull it out, and the hole that's remaining
    is the measure of how you'll be missed.
You may splash all you please when you
    enter.
    You may stir up the water galore.
But stop, and you'll find in a minute
    that it looks quite the same as before.
The moral of this quaint example
    is to do the best that you can.
Be proud of yourself, but remember –
    there is no indispensable man!"

When an individual begins to think he or she is indispensable, there sets in a compulsive and controlling temperament that becomes rather insufferable for others. Hillary of Tours wrote of Christians who suffer from *"irreligiosa sollicitudo pro Deo"* – "a blasphemous anxiety to do God's work for Him!"

The Prodigal Son Who Stayed Home

Some of us are like the elder brother in the story of the
Prodigal Son. We all know about how the younger son
ran away and wasted his wealth and health in pagan
excess. Then, broken and ashamed, he returned to
work as a servant. But the father never gave him the
chance. Instead, he threw a great party and restored
the boy to full privilege as a son!

Meanwhile, back at the ranch ... The elder brother
had a major attitude problem – not only toward the
younger brother, but also toward his father – when,
upon the boy's return, he learned what was happening.

> *"The older brother became angry and refused to go in.
> So his father went out and pleaded with him. But he
> answered his father, 'Look! All these years I've been
> slaving for you and never disobeyed your orders. Yet
> you never gave me even a young goat so I could
> celebrate with my friends. But when this son of yours
> who has squandered your property with prostitutes
> comes home, you kill the fattened calf for him!'"*
> (Luke 15:28–30 NIV)

Oh, what darkness of soul is betrayed here! The elder
son viewed his relationship to his father as *slavery*. Day
after day he ploughed the fields with vengeance, and
plucked the grapes of wrath from the vines with tight-
fisted animosity. Did he feel that he was obligated to
labor so intensely in order to gain his father's favor?
Did he secretly envy the younger brother for running
away from it all? And how did he actually know that

the younger brother had spent his money on prosti-
tutes? He didn't talk to him to find that out; maybe it
was what he secretly desired to do himself!

I've often wondered what would have happened if
the returning prodigal had run into the older brother
before the father saw him in the distance? He probably
would never have made it home.

Also, is it possible that the reason the younger son
ran away in the first place was to get away from his
older brother? I think so. I mean, there is nothing in
the father's manner of speech or conduct that would
explain the boy's decision to run away. He didn't run
away to put distance between him and his father; he
did it to get as far from his older brother as possible! At
least that's how I see it.

And here's a disturbing thought. How many *prodi-
gals* are there in the world today, away from the
Father's house, who left to get away from the *older
brothers* in the Church? And might their reluctance to
return derive from a very real fear of how they will
be treated by those who are "slaving and never dis-
obeying orders?" I shudder to think that the answer is
yes.

Indeed, there are some in the Church like the elder
brother, "slaving" for the Father, so obsessed with
duty that they miss out completely on any delight
they might enjoy in God's house. For such as these the
very thought of "taking a break" and doing nothing is
unthinkable. Poor and wretched souls they are – slaves
and not sons, in their own frightened minds. How
dreadful to live under the delusion that one must
slave for God in order to be accepted by Him. Surely
there is nothing more diabolical than this!

Friend, maybe your dry time is God's way of redeeming you from a false belief that you must always be about the business of ministry in order to be pleasing to Him. Maybe He has heated things up so that you will chill out!

Dry times have a remarkable ability to bring us to the end of our self-motivated efforts and achievements. It is there that we can truly appreciate the words of Jesus, *"apart from Me, you can do nothing"* (John 15:5b NASB)! The desert is a place of rest. We cease from our own works and enter into God's work.

Hidden to Be Revealed

Several years ago John Wimber, a godly man and renowned church leader to whom so many owe so much, had an life-impacting encounter with Christ while in Chicago. Faced with physical exhaustion and spiritual fatigue from long days of relentless ministry, he was at his wits' end. That's when the Lord spoke to his heart these enduring words that forever changed the course of his ministry: "John, I have seen your ministry," the Lord said. "Now, I will show you Mine!" John Wimber was never the same from that moment. The impact he had on thousands of churches regarding worship and ministry to the poor, as well as equipping believers in effectively praying for the sick, is now a matter of church history.

Eighty years ago G.H. Morrison, one of the Church's uncelebrated heroes, wrote:

"It is the glory of God to hide a thing [Proverbs 25:2], and there are many choice places to hide them. He hides silver and gold deep in the heart of the mountains, rubies and diamonds down in the belly of the earth, and pearls in the depths of the sea. But His children, far more precious than all things – them He hides under the shadow of His hand!"

Maybe, dear friend, this dry spell that you've been lamenting is actually the Lord hiding you in the shadow of His hand! Now, what's so bad about *that*?

Chapter 6

Fact No. 4 –

The Desert is a Place of *Restoration*

"Therefore I am now going to allure her;
I will lead her into the desert
and speak tenderly to her.
There I will give her back her vineyards,
and will make the Valley of Achor a door of hope.
There she will sing as in the days of her youth,
as in the day she came up out of Egypt."

(Hosea 2:14–15 NIV)

Restoration is a delightful word, meaning "to give back." There are times in each of our lives when we need restoration – something given back. The Lord sees to it that those times do not pass without our being replenished and strengthened by His grace. In fact, according to Scripture, God actually *allures* us into the desert so He can restore us there.

Matthew Henry comments:

> "By the promise of rest in Christ, we are invited to
> take his yoke upon us; and the work of conversion
> may be forwarded by comforts as well as by
> convictions. But usually the Lord drives us to
> despair of earthly joy and help from ourselves,
> that being shut from every other door, we may
> knock at Mercy's gate."

And of course, to him who knocks the door shall be
opened.

A Fivefold Restoration

Looking at the words of Hosea, we can highlight at
least five specific areas in which we experience restoration during those times when the Lord allures us into
the desert.

The first thing the Lord restores to us during dry
times is our sensitivity to hearing God's voice. He says,
"I will lead her into the desert and speak tenderly to her."
The Hebrew word for "tenderly" literally means
"within." The Lord wants to restore within your heart
the ability to hear His voice.

The desert suits His purposes best in this regard, for
it shuts out all other distractions and tunes your heart
with keen desire to hear what the Lord will say.
Indeed, it brings you to a place where the Lord need
not shout to be heard, but can literally whisper within
you in that same still small voice that made mighty
Elijah cover his face in reverence.

Isaiah said,

> *"He wakens me morning by morning,*
> *wakens my ear to listen like one being taught."*
> (Isaiah 50:4b NIV)

What does it mean to listen *"like one being taught"*? It means to be focused intently upon the one who is speaking, nodding in agreement and making notes of each new discovery. It means to lean forward with pen in hand, and eagerness in your heart, to learn from one who knows what he or she is talking about.

Does this characterize your relationship with the Lord? Are you a student in the classroom of the Holy Spirit? Do you lean into the Lord, longing to hear His voice within, and to do His will without? The dry time will enroll you quicker than almost anything else!

The second thing the Lord restores to us during dry times is our fruitfulness in ministry. He says, *"There I will give her back her vineyards."* The language here is rich in significance. Jesus said:

> *"I am the vine, you are the branches. He who abides in*
> *Me, and I in him, bears much fruit; for without Me you*
> *can do nothing."*   (John 15:5 NKJV)

This shows us that the key to fruitfulness in life is a close abiding relationship with Jesus.

Connected, receptive and effective: these are the three characteristics of an abiding relationship. Like a branch that bears the fruit produced by the Vine, so we must be connected to Christ and receptive to His

Word and His Spirit. This alone will make us effective in what we say and do.

The Lord draws us into dry seasons to strengthen our connection with Him, and our receptivity to His leadership in our lives. His desire is to restore us to a place of great effectiveness.

The third thing the Lord restores to us during dry times is perspective. He says, *"I will make the Valley of Achor a door of hope."* The Hebrew word *achor* means "trouble." It is in the desert – with the Lord – that we discover what we thought was trouble is actually a door of hope! Our perspective has changed.

Job cried,

> *"For the thing which I greatly feared is come upon me."*   (Job 3:25a KJV)

Yet, far from destroying him, Job's epic troubles actually lifted him to another level of life. His story ends with these fable-like words:

> *"Then, when Job prayed for his friends, the Lord restored his wealth and happiness! In fact, the Lord gave him twice as much as before."* (Job 42:10 TLB)

Consider this simple fact: had Job not gone through his difficulties, there would have been no need for the Lord to bless him twice as much as before. The valley of Achor became his door of hope!

Maybe your season of sorrow and loss is actually the Lord's way of positioning you for an even greater blessing than you knew before these troubles came your way. Maybe He has brought you into this desert to restore your perspective, giving you back the ability to see all things – good or bad – from God's redemptive point of view!

The fourth thing the Lord restores to us during dry times is our praise. He says, *"There she will sing as in the days of her youth."* Ah, few voices carry such devotion as those who sing aloud their praise to God fresh from the cradle of conversion!

And then there are those who, having just escaped some dark snare laid for them by Satan, are gathered again in the arms of their Great Savior – breaking out in heavenly anthems of thankful adoration!

How long has it been since you actually *worshipped* the Lord? Oh, I'm not talking about singing songs on Sunday morning, I mean turning toward Him in spirit and truth, to express – sometimes even without words – just how much you love Him, how grateful you are to Him for saving and blessing you.

> "Redeemed how I love to proclaim it!
>   Redeemed by the blood of the Lamb;
> Redeemed thro' His infinite mercy,
>   His child and forever I am.
> I know I shall see in His beauty
>   The king in whose law I delight;
> Who lovingly guardeth my footsteps
>   And giveth me songs in the night!"
>   (Fanny J. Crosby, 1820–1915)

Maybe this dry stretch is orchestrated by the Lord to stir afresh the chords of your slumbering heart, tuning your heart once again to join with the chorus of heaven's ransomed as they sing the glad songs of Zion!

The fifth thing the Lord restores to us during dry times is our liberty. He says, *"as in the day she came up out of Egypt."* The story of the children of Israel in the land of Egypt, under the bondage of Pharaoh, is known throughout the world. The cruelty of their oppressors, the mystery of the Ten Plagues, the surrender of Pharaoh to the will of God, and the parting of the Red Sea – all these things stir our souls deeply.

These themes are found in our own salvation. We can recall just as vividly how it was when the Lord first broke the power of sin in our lives, and set us free to live without guilt, shame or fear. We can also tell of our own manna, wondrously supplied, of the shade by day and the fire by night, and how the water gushed out of the rock which was struck with a rod.

But, like the Israelites, perhaps over time we ourselves have drifted away from our deep affections and tenacious devotion. Maybe the prosperity of our own Promised Land caused our hearts to cool and our heads to swell, while our hands grew idle and our feet aimless. Maybe we have somehow been overtaken by other masters, who now contain us within a prison called Compromise, and subtly destroy us through our own passivity and indifference.

Ah! It's just then that the Lord allures us into the desert, that He may work within us a measure of His grace that restores the freedom we had *"in the day* [we] *came up out of Egypt."*

A Final Thought

The Lord says, *"I will lead her into the desert."* If you are going through a dry time, don't think for a moment that God has forsaken you or forgotten you. He has done neither. In fact, He is the very One who has orchestrated this season in order to restore multiple blessings back into your life.

While you may feel miles away, cut off and forgotten, you are closer to the Lord than perhaps you have ever been! He didn't *banish* you into this dry place – He *allured* you there! No matter how you look at it, this has implications of romance and intimacy. Rejoice, therefore, and encourage yourself in the Lord just as David did:

> *"Why are you downcast, O my soul?*
> *Why so disturbed within me?*
> *Put your hope in God,*
> *for I will yet praise him,*
> *my Savior and my God."*   (Psalm 42:11 NIV)

Chapter 7

Fact No. 5 –

The Desert
is a Place of *Preparation*

"A voice of one calling:
'In the desert prepare
   *the way for the L*ORD*!'"*   (Isaiah 40:3a NIV)

Years ago, during a time when the church I pastored was too small to afford me a salary, I took a job in a paint and body shop as a painter's helper. My duties were menial – sweeping up the shop, taking out the trash, running to the store, and a host of other odd jobs nobody else wanted to do.

My primary role was doing the preparatory work – getting a car ready for the painter to finish. On any day you would find me cleaning, sanding, taping, applying primer, repairing scratches and minor dents, and setting up the paint booth for the painter. After the paint had been applied and cured, I then had the responsibility of untaping, reassembling and finishing out the job for an on-time delivery to the customer. The work was laborious, dirty, frustrating, time-consuming and seldom ever appreciated. Certainly the customers were thrilled with the finished product, and the painter received many a pat on the back for a job well done. But I never recall anyone ever commenting about the preparation work – unless, of course, the work was done wrong.

The finished product was always spectacular and, in a few instances, award-winning. But the preparation process was invariably pure grunt and grief. It only took about fifteen minutes of actual work to paint a car, but it took three to four days to get it ready. Oh, how I wanted to be the *painter!*

The painter worked up front, greeting customers and hobnobbing with the boss. The painter's helper was hidden away in the back of the shop, reeking of paint fumes and muttering to himself.

During my time at this job, I learned that no matter how skilled the painter was in applying the paint and polishing the finish, if the prep work was faulty, it *always* showed through. Therefore, great pains were taken (and given) in the preparation process.

Are you beginning to get the picture? The work of preparation, though often unpleasant, is absolutely vital! And while it was the finished product that always won approval, it was the prep work in those long hours of *un*noticed labor that made it all possible. Without the prep work there is no unveiling.

Might the same apply to our lives?

The Final Cut

Have you ever seen a paring knife? It is usually small, handy, and very sharp. Its purpose is to cut the flesh of the fruit away from the tough, tangy skin so that its sweetness can be enjoyed to the full.

To pare is to cut. *Pre*pare means to cut beforehand (like a tailor-made garment). Might this be what God is up to in your life during this dry time you are experiencing? Could He be cutting away the tough, unwanted bits of your life? Jesus said,

> *" . . . every branch that does bear fruit he prunes so that it will be even more fruitful."* (John 15:2 NIV)

Don't let this pass too quickly without appreciating the promise in the midst of the pain. He said that the pruning of the branch is so that *"it will be even more fruitful."* You have *been* fruitful in the past, and you will *be* even more fruitful in the future. Give God time to make the final cut, and even co-operate with Him in the process.

A Highway in the Wilderness

Isaiah said,

> *"make straight in the wilderness a highway for our God."* (Isaiah 40:3b NIV)

Perhaps God has placed you in the wilderness to make a path ready for the Lord. Maybe there are things that need to happen *in* your life to prepare you for what God wants to happen *through* your life. Maybe this dry time you are in is God's way of drawing you away from what you are doing, so He can take you into what He can do.

Often God hides us away in the interest of larger service. He must first draw us away from the things we are doing, in order to draw us to the better thing He has for us to do.

Years ago Jack Taylor taught me to pray,

"Lord, do in me anything You need to do, so You can do through me everything You want to do!"

I highly recommend this prayer to you. The Lord will not fail to answer it thoroughly.

Isaiah continues:

"Every valley shall be raised up,
every mountain and hill made low;
the rough ground shall become level,
the.rugged places a plain."   (Isaiah 40:4 NIV)

The purpose of this massive overhaul, this earth-moving endeavor, is to build a highway for God so that the glory of the Lord may be revealed.

"And the glory of the LORD will be revealed,
and all mankind together will see it.
For the mouth of the LORD has spoken."
                                    (Isaiah 40:5 NIV)

Could it be that the Lord wants to reveal His glory in and through you? But in order to do so, He must first prepare you in the wilderness.

And think about this. The wilderness is the last place civilized people would ever look for God. Yet, that's where He is most often to be found. It suits Him to take the things of no value, and make something of nothing. That which is despised by human beings is highly esteemed by God.

John the Baptist was in the wilderness until *"he appeared publicly to Israel"* (Luke 1:80; the KJV says *"till the day of his shewing unto Israel"*). Maybe this dry time of yours is similar, and perhaps one day the Lord will bring you into the public arena too. Perhaps.

My encouragement to you is not to despair during these times of lethargic duty and unrewarded faithfulness – God is indeed up to something special. You will thank Him profusely when the day comes that you see it.

I think of Naomi and her great sorrow during a time of famine and loss. The drought and famine in Israel drove her to the land of Moab. There her husband and two sons died, leaving her with two daughters-in-law who were Moabites. When she decided to return to Israel, Ruth insisted on staying with her. Naomi told Ruth,

> *"Oh, how I grieve for you that the Lord has punished me in a way that injures you."*   (Ruth 1:13 TLB)

This is an unusual point of view. The bitterness of Naomi's heart hindered her from thinking clearly, and caused her to speak things that were not true. The fact is that the Lord did not punish her at all; rather, He brought her through her trials to a place of great honor and blessing for both herself and Ruth.

You see, Ruth became the wife of Boaz, father of Obed, who was the father of Jesse, the father of David. This placed Naomi in the royal lineage of the Lord Jesus Christ. Her "dry time" proved to be the very means of a profound and enriching work of God on her behalf. She thought God was punishing her. Instead, He was preparing her for a place in history! The Apostle Paul said it best,

> "... the sufferings of this present time are not worthy to be compared with the glory which shall be revealed in us."   (Romans 8:18 NKJV)

Things Aren't Always What They Seem

There is a delightful little story of two angels who stopped to spend the night in the home of a wealthy family. The family was rude and refused to let the angels stay in the guest room. Instead they were given a small space in the cold basement. As they made their bed on the hard floor, the older angel saw a hole in the wall and repaired it. When the younger angel asked why, the older angel replied, "Things aren't always what they seem."

The next night the two angels came to rest at the house of a very poor, but very hospitable farmer and his wife. After sharing what little food they had, the couple let the angels sleep in their bed where they could have a good night's rest. When the sun came up the next morning, the angels found the farmer and his wife in tears. Their only cow, whose milk had been their sole income, lay dead in the field.

The younger angel was infuriated and asked the older angel, "How could you have let this happen? The first man had everything, yet you helped him. The second family had little but was willing to share everything, and you let the cow die."

"Things aren't always what they seem," the older angel replied. "When we stayed in the basement of the mansion, I noticed there was gold stored in that hole in the wall. Since the owner was so obsessed with greed and unwilling to share his good fortune, I sealed the wall so he wouldn't find it. Then last night as we slept in the farmer's bed, the angel of death came for his wife. I gave him the cow instead."

You see, things aren't always what they seem. The Bible promises us that

> "...all things work together for good, to those who love God, to those who are called according to His purpose." (Romans 8:28 NKJV)

Surely you can trust the Lord to work things out for your good during this dry time.

The Land of In-between

Earlier we discussed how the Lord called the disciples to a desert place to get some rest. They had seen great ministry *prior* to their desert experience. And, as a matter of fact, they went on to even greater ministry *after* the desert experience was finished. From this we learn that the desert place in the life of disciples is located *in-between* ministry! Could it be that if you are presently experiencing a dry time, then the Lord is getting ready to call you into a more effective ministry than you have known?

As we have seen, John the Baptist *"lived in the desert until he appeared publicly to Israel"* (Luke 1:80 NIV). I wonder if John ever thought, "How long must I endure this blasted heat, these stringy locusts' legs, and this rocky waste land!? I'm the prophet of the Most High! Let's get this show on the road!"

I wonder if Moses ever wondered how long he would tend sheep in Midian, or if Paul, while making tents in Tarsus, wondered if he would ever get a chance to preach about the unsearchable riches of Christ. I wonder what Joseph thought in the prison of Egypt, or David in the cave of Adullam, or Daniel in the courts of Babylon, or Jeremiah in Jonathan's dungeon, or John on the Isle of Patmos.

It seems that God takes all of us through these times of darkness, dryness, dullness, dreariness and dread. You are not alone, my friend. Look around and see if any of these champions left you some words of hope scrawled on the walls!

Years ago – during a dramatic season of evangelism known as the 'Jesus Movement' – I was on the front lines in many spiritual campaigns, and saw the Lord do extraordinary things. There seemed no end in sight as we met daily and celebrated scores of new converts to Christ. But then an odd thing happened to me on my way to destiny. The river dried up. Everything seemed to come to an abrupt halt, and I found myself sidelined while life apparently went on without me. I remember walking the streets in my neighborhood late into the evening, crying out to God. With tears streaming down my cheeks I would ask, "Lord, are you *ever* going to use me?" Now I look in astonishment at some of the things that God has done.

Friend, I know the same will be true for you. This desert you are in, this dry time you are going through, is a season of preparation. The Lord is fitting you for something yet to come. You are not ready for it, and it is not ready for you. The best thing that can happen is for you to grow and become strong in spirit while you are in this wilderness. In God's good time, He will move you from the Land of In-between and "show you to Israel."

Count on it!

Chapter 8

Is That Your *Final* Answer?

"I cried out to God for help;
I cried out to God to hear me.
When I was in distress, I sought the LORD;
at night I stretched out untiring hands
and my soul refused to be comforted.
I remembered you, O God, and I groaned;
I mused, and my spirit grew faint."

(Psalm 77:1–3 NIV)

There are some questions for which there are no answers. For example, why isn't "phonics" spelled the way it sounds? Or, why do animal rights' activists spray paint on the fur coats of women, but not on the leather jackets of motorcycle gangs?

Or, how come Superman could stop bullets with his chest, but always ducked when someone threw a gun at him? What happens if you get scared half-to-death *twice*? Why doesn't glue stick to the inside of the bottle? And what do birds see when *they* get knocked unconscious?

Or, why is there an expiriration date on sour cream?
Why do kamikaze pilots wear helmets? And if you're
born again, do you have *two* belly buttons? Is atheism
a non-prophet foundation? And, why have we never
read this headline "Psychic Wins Lottery!"

We may never know! It seems that there are just
some questions that have no answers.

Maybe you have made it this far in this book, and
still don't have an answer for *your* questions. Maybe
you're convinced that there is no help for you, that
God doesn't even know you exist. Maybe you're
beginning to wonder if *He* even exists.

Ages ago, the Psalmist Asaph experienced the same
thing while enduring his own dry time.

> *"I found myself in trouble and went looking for my
>   Lord;*
>   *my life was an open wound that wouldn't heal.*
> *When friends said, 'Everything will turn out all
>   right,'*
>   *I didn't believe a word they said.*
> *I remember God – and shake my head.*
>   *I bow my head – then wring my hands.*
> *I'm awake all night – not a wink of sleep;*
>   *I can't even say what's bothering me.*
> *I go over the days one by one,*
>   *I ponder the years gone by.*
> *I strum my lute all through the night,*
>   *wondering how to get my life together."*
>   (Psalm 77:2–5 *The Message*)

There are a few choice lines in what we just read that
warrant a closer look. For instance, *"I found myself in*

trouble and went looking for my Lord." Why is it that we don't look for the Lord *until* we find ourselves in trouble? Why does it so often take distress to drive us to the Lord? Why do we live our lives with Him in the background until disaster strikes? Doesn't He deserve better than that from us?

Here is another very telling remark: *"my life was an open wound that wouldn't heal."* The old King James Bible puts it this way, *"my soul refused to be comforted."* Dry times can do that to you.

A sick man turns away from even the most nourishing food. Spurgeon wrote,

> "Many a daughter of despondency has pushed aside the cup of gladness, and many a son of sorrow has hugged his chains."

Perhaps you are even now in such a dark place. Maybe your soul is in such distress that you find no comfort – even if the Lord Himself served it up on a silver platter.

Here's another great line from our psalm: *"I can't even say what's bothering me."* Have you ever felt this way, unable to put your finger on exactly what it is that's wrong? Do you feel like this now? Isn't it at least somewhat comforting for you to know that a great man of prayer like Asaph went through the same experience ages ago? That should let you know that it's not just you. We *all* experience this bewildering feeling from time to time.

Here is one more line worth noting, *"I strum my lute all through the night, wondering how to get my life together."* What a picture of desperate quietness! Sleepless and speechless, reduced to great extremities, randomly strumming in the night while the mind wanders aimlessly down the back roads of scrambled thought.

Is there *anybody* out there?

Hey, God, Don't You Even Care!

In his desert experience, Asaph cries aloud what each of us have wondered during our own dry times. Erupting from his soul is a volley of questions asked by saints through the ages:

> *"Will the Lord reject for ever?*
> *Will he never show his favor again?*
> *Has his unfailing love vanished for ever?*
> *Has his promise failed for all time?*
> *Has God forgotten to be merciful?*
> *Has he in anger withheld his compassion?"*
> (Psalm 77:7–9 NIV)

Have you ever questioned God?

You know what I mean. During a particularly trying time, when nothing made sense – and all hell was breaking loose – did you ever look up to heaven and ask God to speak to you? What happened?

Probably nothing.

Years ago the cartoon strip, Broom Hilda, showed the witch looking up to heaven, asking, "God, is there any chance of me getting into heaven?" The next frame showed a great fist coming out of the clouds. SMASH! And then in the final frame we see the flattened Broom Hilda muttering out of the dust, "So, shall I take that as a *'No'*?"

Or how about the time Charlie Brown asked, "Why is all this happening to me?" And a voice from heaven replied, *"Why not?"*

Seeing the forthrightness of Asaph's inquiries, apparently it's okay with the Lord that we ask Him tough questions. In fact, it may be mandatory, especially if *not* asking them means being dishonest with our own soul. Like the Queen of Sheba before Solomon, proving him with hard questions (see 1 Kings 10:1), we too may ask questions of the Lord concerning anything that is troubling us.

But is it okay with us if He does not answer? Or, if He gives an answer other than what we want to hear? Let me ask you this: *Is He still God even when your questions have no answers at all?*

We ask God many questions and often receive no reply. The more desperate our circumstances, and the more earnest our inquiries – the more bewildered we are by His silence. If such a silence be prolonged, we may even allow a root of bitterness into our hearts which defiles our faith and darkens our thoughts with mockery against God Himself. "Is this Your final answer?" we fire into heaven. "If so, then I don't care to trust You any more." Perhaps it would serve a nobler purpose if we could hear God speak – even if it was just one more time. Perhaps we may hear Him turn the table and ask us, "Is this *your* final answer?" Isn't that the real question we are faced with when Heaven is silent in our seasons of spiritual drought?

Augustus Tholuck wrote,

> "There are moments in the lives of all believers when God and His ways become unintelligible to them. They get lost in profound meditation, and nothing is left them but a despondent sigh."

How then should we respond when Heaven's final answer is silence? Bill Gaither summed it up best in the words of the beloved Gospel song:

> "I long so much to feel the touch
> that others seem to know.
> But if I never feel a thing
> I'll trust You even so.
> I believe; help Thou my unbelief.
> I step into the unknown, trusting
>   like a child."

James Smith, a contemporary of Spurgeon, wrote,

> "God has provided suitable and sufficient comfort for His people. He sends them comforters just as their circumstances require. But they at times refuse to hear the voice of the messenger.
>
> The Lord has perhaps taken away an idol, or He withholds His sensible presence that we may learn to live by faith, or He has blighted their worldly prospects, or He has written vanity and emptiness upon all their delights.
>
> They give way to passion, as did Jonah. Or yield to extreme sorrow, as did Rachel. Or fall under the

power of temptation, or accept the notion that they have no right to be comforted. This is wrong; decidedly wrong.

Look at what is left to you! Behold what the Gospel presents to you! Consider what heaven will be to you!"

(*Treasury of David*, Psalm LXXVII, p. 418)

Paul assures us that

" ... *the sufferings of this present time are not worthy to be compared with the glory which shall be revealed in us.*" (Romans 8:18 NKJV)

In another place he says,

"*For our light affliction, which is but for a moment, is working for us a far more exceeding and eternal weight of glory, while we do not look at the things which are seen, but at the things which are not seen. For the things which are seen are temporary, but the things which are not seen are eternal.*"

(2 Corinthians 4:17–18 NKJV)

It seems that the solution is found by setting your sights higher than earth's limited boundaries. The eye of faith must pierce the veil of time and space, and peer into eternity, finding the faithfulness of God's unfailing love to be the sure tonic for each affliction of soul and mind.

God's Answer to Man's Dry Time Dilemma

Asaph, having penned for us the basic struggle of the soul in times of darkness and dryness, now finishes his psalm by mapping out the pathway to hope and restoration – even when God does not answer.

> *"I will call to mind the deeds of the LORD;*
> *I will remember your wonders of old.*
> *I will meditate on all your work,*
> *And muse on your mighty deeds.*
> *Your way, O God, is holy.*
> *What god is so great as our God?*
> *You are the God who works wonders;*
> *You have displayed your might among the peoples."*
> (Psalm 77:11–14 NRSV)

I recall the time when King David was plundered by his enemies and forsaken by his friends. It happened at a place called Ziklag. Caught in that solitary moment of unimaginable peril, when even his choicest soldiers and dearest followers were turning against him in a murderous rage, David found a way out of his distress. The Bible tells us:

> *"Now David was greatly distressed, for the people spoke of stoning him, because the soul of all the people was grieved, every man for his sons and his daughters. But David strengthened himself in the LORD his God."*
> (1 Samuel 30:6 NKJV)

The word "strengthened" comes from a Hebrew word meaning "to fasten upon; to seize, fortify and withstand; to encourage oneself to continue" (*Strong's Exhaustive Concordance of the Bible*, no. 2388). David rallied to the Lord and lifted his soul above the peril of his circumstances. He then rallied his people, by the sheer strength of his redeemed will, to trust the Lord and rise up with Him against the enemy. They did, and the Lord brought a great victory to His people that day. It was, in fact, the turning point in David's life. From there, he went on to become the King of all Israel.

Here is my point: indeed, my recommendation to you in your own dark night of sorrow, while you endure your own desperate stretch of dry spiritual tundra. Follow the example of both David and Asaph. Recall, even now, the many times the Lord has answered you. Remind your soul of the countless times He has been gracious to you and blessed you with that real sense of His presence that turns the darkest moment into heaven itself.

Think of the times – even if you can only remember one – when the joy of the Lord was your strength. Remember how it has been for you in the house of the Lord, worshipping with the saints in beautiful assembly. Remember hearing the great and glorious Word of God proclaimed by His anointed messenger, and feeling the power of His Holy Spirit move upon your very being.

Call to mind those former days when you were filled with faith unshakable and bold as a lion in your witness for Christ. Remember afresh the many tears you have cried at the joy of seeing friends and loved ones come to trust Christ as Savior and Lord.

Surely you can testify that the Lord, your God, has indeed been good and gracious to you. Surely the clouds are not so thick, and the burden so heavy, that you are altogether robbed of remembrance. Surely in all your thoughts there remains at least one fond recall of a tender and treasured moment with Jesus.

Now consider this. He did all these things for you, knowing that *this* day of trial would come, knowing these brooding questions about His love and faithfulness would rise in your heart. It did not stop Him from showing you His love then, nor does it stop Him from giving you His love now!

Come on, Child of God, encourage yourself in the Lord!

Epilogue

"The desert and the parched land will be glad;
  the wilderness will rejoice and blossom.
Like the crocus, it will burst into bloom;
  it will rejoice greatly and shout for joy.
The glory of Lebanon will be given to it,
  the splendor of Carmel and Sharon;
they will see the glory of the LORD,
  the splendor of our God.
Strengthen the feeble hands,
  steady the knees that give way;
say to those with fearful hearts,
  'Be strong, do not fear;
your God will come,
  he will come with vengeance;
with divine retribution
  he will come to save you.'
Then will the eyes of the blind be opened
  and the ears of the deaf unstopped.
Then will the lame leap like a deer,
  and the mute tongue shout for joy.

Water will gush forth in the wilderness
and streams in the desert.
The burning sand will become a pool,
the thirsty ground bubbling springs.
In the haunts where jackals once lay,
grass and reeds and papyrus will grow.
And a highway will be there;
it will be called the Way of Holiness.
The unclean will not journey on it;
it will be for those who walk in that Way;
wicked fools will not go about on it.
No lion will be there,
nor will any ferocious beast get up on it;
they will not be found there.
But only the redeemed will walk there,
and the ransomed of the Lord *will return.*
They will enter Zion with singing;
everlasting joy will crown their heads.
Gladness and joy will overtake them,
and sorrow and sighing will flee away."

(Isaiah 35:1–10 NIV)

Throughout this book we have discovered many positive things about going through the dry times. It turns out that what we generally thought was awful is actually full of awe.

We have seen that the desert is a place of testing, in the positive sense of the word. That it is a place of growth, a place of rest, a place of restoration, and a place of preparation.

In conclusion, and to sum it all up into one general confession – especially in the light of Isaiah's amazing prophecy – we are assured by God that the desert is a place of promise!

If you are in a season of dryness, barrenness, or ineffectiveness, a time when the Lord seems not to care, and when your dreams and hopes of service fall powerless to the ground – then rest assured. You are exactly where the Lord wants you for now – and in His good time the desert and parched land will be glad . . . and sorrow and sighing will flee away.

Sermon Outline

The following outline is provided for those who would like to preach or teach this message in their church or Bible Study group.

May God bless you and your hearers!

GOING THROUGH THE DRY TIMES

Text: Psalm 63:1–4 (NIV)

"A psalm of David. When he was in the Desert of Judah.

"O God, you are my God,
  earnestly I seek you;
my soul thirsts for you,
  my body longs for you,
in a dry and weary land
  where there is no water.
I have seen you in the sanctuary
  and beheld your power and your glory.
Because your love is better than life,
  my lips will glorify you.
I will praise you as long as I live,
  and in your name I will lift up my hands."

Introduction

There is an unmistakable move of the Holy Spirit happening in the world today. A remarkable characteristic of this particular season of blessing is its *diversity*.

- Toronto and Pensacola
- Promise Keepers and Women of Faith
- Rocking the Nations and world evangelism
- Argentina, Brazil, and England revival
- The Alpha Course

- Increase in worship and ministry
- Integrity in the pulpit, and power in the Church
- Reconciliation (racial and denominational).

Any one of these would be sign enough of the presence and power of the Holy Spirit – but when one considers that they are occurring simultaneously, it is a staggering move of God!

One might conclude that the whole Church is caught up in this visitation of God. But the fact is many followers of Christ – perhaps the great majority – are experiencing something altogether different. It is yet another example of the diversity of God's work in our midst, and may in fact be the most bewildering sign of them all.

I call it: *Going through the dry times.*

- Pass me not, O Gentle Savior!
- You've gone here and there and not found it – and the one time you decide not to go ... that's the time when the glory of God falls!
- You have prayed, cried, pledged, hoped, hopped, danced, given and waited earnestly for the Lord to zap you ... and still nothing has happened.
- Boy, have I got news for you!

A Note of Clarification

It is important that I take a moment to explain what we do not mean when we talk about going through the dry times:

- Not the dread that is caused by unconfessed sins (see Psalm 31:9–10 and Psalm 32:3–6).

- Not the dearth that is caused by burn out (this is a self-inflicted state, brought on by compulsive duty).

- Not the drought that is caused by neglect and indifference.

If you recognize yourself as being caught in any one of these conditions, I say, turn to the Lord and you will find Him rich in mercy and ready to forgive and restore.

Now, then, onward through this desert land!

1. The Song of the Desert of Judah

(a) David's praise was suited to his circumstance. If you are in a desert, it should not silence your praise to God; rather it should define it.

(b) His song encompassed
    (i) *present:* I am in a dry and weary land
    (ii) *past:* I have seen your power and your glory
    (iii) *future:* I will lift up my hands in your name.

(c) This shows that we go *through* the dry times; we are never left *in* them!

(d) The Desert of *Judah* (isn't that *in* the Promised Land?).

2. A Lesson for Us Today

(a) 1 Corinthians 10:11 – *"written for our instruction."*

(b) There is a desert in *our* Promised Land.

    (i) A common experience for all believers

       • Moses, Elijah, David, Paul

       • Jesus Himself was *"led by the Spirit into the desert"* (Matthew 4:1).

    (ii) Common also is how easily we misunderstand the purposes of God during these dry times when the lights go out (see Isaiah 50:10–11).

(c) *"You will know the truth."*

Permit me to show you Five Uplifting Truths about *going through the dry times.* Knowing these truths will help you navigate your way through the dry and weary land to that city whose builder and maker is God!

FIVE FACTS ABOUT THE DESERT EXPERIENCE IN THE LIVES OF BELIEVERS

Fact No. 1 –
The Desert is a Place of *Testing*

1. Deuteronomy 8:2

    (a) God *led* them in the desert.

    (b) His purpose was to prove them – not to Him, but to themselves!

    (c) He also wanted to prove Himself to them.

(d) God often puts us in situations that are too much for us, so that we will learn there is no situation that is too much for Him!

2. Share a personal example of passing a test.

Fact No. 2 –
The Desert is a Place of *Growth*

1. Luke 1:80
   (a) God is never in a hurry; He wants us to grow up in all things into Christ.
   (b) The desert suits His purposes well.
      (i) We are weaned and made humble – Psalm 131:1–2.
      (ii) Our spirit is made strong – Luke 1:80.
      (iii) We are eventually brought forth in God's timing.
         • Joseph in Egypt
         • Moses in Midian
         • David in Adullam
         • John the Baptist
         • Paul the Apostle
   (c) Jesus is our best example – Luke 2:52.
      (i) He grew in four significant ways:
         • Mentally
         • Physically
         • Spiritually
         • Socially

(ii) Seven facts about healthy growth:

- Healthy things grow.
- Growing things change.
- Changing things challenge us.
- Challenge forces us to trust God.
- Trust leads to obedience.
- Obedience makes us healthy.
- Healthy things grow.

Perhaps this short poem says it best for all of us:

"Light after darkness, gain after loss;
    Strength after weakness, crown after cross;
Sweet after bitter, hope after fears;
    Home after wandering, praise after tears;
Sheaves after sowing, sun after rain;
    Sight after mystery, peace after pain;
Joy after sorrow, calm after blast;
    Rest after weariness, sweet rest at last;
Near after distance, gleam after gloom;
    Love after loneliness, life after tomb;
After long agony, rapture of bliss;
    Right was the pathway, leading to this."

(Anon)

Fact No. 3 –
The Desert is a Place of *Rest*

1. Mark 6:31

(a) Come apart, before you come apart!

(i) The Lord knows our limits.

(ii) He also knows our vanity.

(b) The prodigal son who stayed home.

(i) An attitude problem

- toward his brother
- toward his father
- toward himself.

(ii) A slave and not a son.

2. Proverbs 25:2

(a) It is the glory of God to hide a thing.

(b) Maybe He is hiding you in the palm of His hand!

Fact No. 4 –
The Desert is a Place of *Restoration*

1. Hosea 2:14–15

(a) Restoration: to give back.

(b) Hosea highlights five specific areas in which we experience restoration during our dry times:

(i) Our sensitivity to God's voice – *"I will . . . speak tenderly to her."*

(ii) Our fruitfulness in ministry – *"I will give her back her vineyards."*

(iii) Our perspective – *"[I] will make the valley of Achor a door of hope."*

(iv) Our praise – *"There she will sing as in the days of her youth . . . "*

(v) Our liberty – *"as in the day she came up out of Egypt."*

2. "I will allure her..."

    (a) The Lord has not banished you to the desert ... He has allured you there!

    (b) Anyway you look at it, the word "allure" carries definite implications of intimacy and romance.

    (c) You've never been closer to the Lord than right now.

Fact No. 5 –
The Desert is a Place of *Preparation*

1. Isaiah 40:3

    (a) *"In the desert prepare the way for the Lord."*

        (i) Preparation is always a long and often unappreciated process.

        (ii) Without it, there is no finished product.

    (b) The Final Cut

        (i) Prepare: to cut beforehand.

        (ii) Tailor-made by the Lord.

2. Isaiah's promise

    (a) A massive overhaul – every valley, mountain, rough place and crooked way.

    (b) A monumental revelation – *"the glory of the* LORD *will be revealed!"*

3. Things aren't always what they seem

    (a) John the Baptist in the wilderness

    (b) Naomi in the land of Moab

    (c) Moses in Midian

(d) Paul in Tarsus

(e) Joseph in Egypt

(f) Daniel in Babylon

(g) Jeremiah in the dungeon

(h) John on the Isle of Patmos

(i) YOU – in the desert.

Conclusion

Read Isaiah 35:1–10.

* *The desert is a place of promise!*

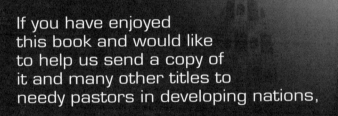

If you have enjoyed
this book and would like
to help us send a copy of
it and many other titles to
needy pastors in developing nations,

please write for further information,
or send your gift to:

Sovereign World Trust
PO Box 777
Tonbridge
Kent TN11 0ZS
United Kingdom

www.sovereignworldtrust.com